Death
Will
Be
Our
Curfew

Death

Will

Be

Our

Curfew

POEMS

Amber Showalter

Published by Grown-Up Punk Publications, Harrisonburg, VA

Edited and designed by Girl Friday Productions
www.girlfridayproductions.com

Cover design: Emily Weigel
Interior design: Paul Barrett
Project management: Kristin Duran
Editorial management: Bethany Davis
Image credits: cover © Shutterstock/Juri V, Shutterstock/Brilliant Eye

ISBN (paperback): 979-8-9861689-0-6
ISBN (e-book): 979-8-9861689-1-3

Library of Congress Control Number: 2022911529

To those who were gone to all along.

To those who lost their lives in these pages—
Michael, Randy, Tim, Mrs. H, the seven patients of Seasons,
the lost ghost of Ashes.
These words would not exist without your existence,
and they will forever serve their purpose to keep your memory
and your love alive.

To those who currently find themselves
lost somewhere in the stages of grief—
whether it's 8:15 p.m. or almost midnight—
I hope these words meet you where you're at
and help you along the rest of the way.

To those who mourn the little things—
expired emotions, the passing of seasons, pieces of yourself—
to grief, these things are not small at all.
I hope this book joins you on your path
and helps to make each day a bit lighter.
Stay as long as you need to—
even if it keeps you out a little past curfew.

CONTENTS

8 P.M.

HELLO, MY NAME IS . . .

At age 26, I had graduated from nursing school and was moving to a new city to begin my career. It would be my very first attempt at saving the world. In between the formalities of paperwork, packing and panicking, I managed to visit my gym one last time in the days preceding my move.

One of the regular *Hi, how are you today?* gym-goers approached me and struck up some small talk, and in passing I mentioned I was moving in the following days to pursue my career.

You're leaving? he responded. *That sucks. I mean, congratulations and everything, but I just hate it when regulars leave. I don't think I even know your name, it's just nice to see the same people every day.*

Oh, well, my name is . . . , I began.

No, he interrupted. *I don't want to know it. I know your face. And that's enough. Best of luck to you.*

I walked away from the conversation somewhat astounded, mentally acknowledging that this must be the most poignant goodbye I had ever received from a random stranger.

I proceeded with moving, and within weeks discovered that I hated my job. It was my first taste of healthcare as an industry, as a business, with the main players—the patients and the healthcare workers—on the bottom rung of the ladder, constantly left to juggle the logistics of bullshit, with no time or resources to actually care about anyone.

Needless to say, I did not save the world. I did not save anyone's world. I moved back home.

At 27, I got married.

At 28, I was slammed into walls, cheated on and nearly killed.

At 29, I divorced.

At 30, I had been happily living on my own, working at a local hospital in a job I loved.

One day, I was floated to a different unit for the shift. The cancer unit. This unit was always hard. It carried with it the aura of a heartbreaking sadness in a revolving-door fashion. I sucked up my sad, put on a fake smile and headed in to report.

He just found out yesterday, the off-going nurse said of the 40-something-year-old patient with a newly discovered mass. I felt the aura creep back in as I entered the patient's room to introduce myself.

Hey, I know you! exclaimed the 40-something-year-old patient, and I realized it was *Hi, how are you today?* gym-goer lying in the bed in front of me.

How are you?! I responded. *I'll be your nurse today, my name is . . .* I paused, remembering our previous conversation. *My name is Amber,* I finished, knowing I had no choice—patients need to know the name of their nurse—but also realizing I couldn't grant the one request he had ever asked of me in his entire life.

Throughout the shift, we spent any extra minutes I had catching up. We talked about the gym, the life I had left for and subsequently come back from, and his pending biopsy.

It was a difficult shift for both of us, as he went for test after test, results pending but not looking promising. By the end of the day, his parents had stopped by. It wasn't long before they were crying, he was crying, and as he was wheeled to the operating room for his biopsy, I too, was choking back tears. The overwhelming aura of heaviness hovered, and I couldn't shake it—things like this are not supposed to happen to people you know.

While he and his parents were away for his procedure and his room was empty, I went in to ensure that things were tidy and in order before the next shift arrived. In midst of my half-assed organization attempt, I noticed a soda bottle on his bedside table. I glanced at the label.

Share a Coke with Amber, it said.

A wry smile found its way to my face, and the dark aura was joined by irony as I turned off the harsh overhead light and left for the day.

BIRDS OF PREY

Spring has sprung in this beautiful ghost town
cherry blossoms bloom, it's a lovely sight
as we assess the collateral damage
to see who has survived the night

The sun rises just past the wire fence
as I pass by a stranger, I hold my breath
he isn't aware of the power I possess
being a blonde-haired, blue-eyed harbinger of death

Below the biggest star on the horizon
this wish as a prayer without an amen
strip me this day of this power
and let us all begin again

The birds of prey are circling
I've got vultures in my head
waiting on the homicide of time
and the things that haven't happened yet

They perch on picket fences
clawed-grip melancholy, stuck like a virus
black figures against the rising sun
casting ominous shadows across my iris

But wait
maybe there's a saving grace
and a little false hope
before we go

With their arms outstretched
their shadows kind of looked like angel wings
as the wind passed by phantom vocal cords to whisper,
Don't worry, baby. You won't feel a thing.

No one will know it was you
look at all this living you have yet to undo
through outstretched wings, time and grace
you can console all your victims in a better place

But one blink and they're gone
these feathered false brandishers of hope
I walk on and feign I heard nothing
as I brush off the tickle in my throat

The sun rises just past the wire fence
as I pass by a stranger, I hold my breath
he isn't aware of the power I possess
being a blonde-haired, blue-eyed harbinger of death

The birds of prey are circling
I've got vultures in my head
waiting on the homicide of time
and the things that haven't happened yet

The birds of prey
are circling

I've got vultures in my head

ASHES, ASHES

It's been passed down through the years
that *Ring Around the Rosie*
is about the Black Plague.
Oh, how happily we sang it as kids—
dancing around in a circle, falling down,
getting back up and repeating—
knowing very little about what we were actually singing.

There is no getting back up in *Ring Around the Rosie*.
Falling down is forever,
and the ashes are permanent.

Now we cite end times
when we have no better explanation for the world around us.
Step outside.
Even the air is poison.
We inhale our demise,
and with an aura of invincibility
we go about our boring chores,
intentionally oblivious to the fact that we could ever fall down.

All the bad—
those are things that happen to other people.
It's a near-miss story,
a friend-of-a-friend,
a two-minute-old car accident on the highway.
Things like that don't happen to us.
They happen to someone else.

But let me tell you—
we are not invincible.
This will come for you,
eventually.
Everyone is someone's someone else.
You are someone's someone else.
And so am I.

Our bleeding ignorance,
willful intolerance
and fearless casualty—
even the ghosts should be afraid of us.
For how many of them have we left behind,
wandering hospital hallways and nursing home corridors,
singing softly—

ashes, ashes

—waiting,
watching the next person die alone as they did.

They peer out windows,
identifying with our shadows on the ground
as what they once looked like
when they were alive.
They remember being a shadow
under unflattering fluorescent light
as they pulled away from their body,
and hid cowering in the closet.
They just couldn't take being beat on
during that last round of CPR,
couldn't stand the muffled shouts through face masks in the room
and the splattering of blood all over plastic shields,
couldn't stand the dizziness of spinning around the room
in circles above their body,
hearing a chorus of whispering shadows around them—

ashes, ashes.

When everyone in the room
throws their hands up in defeat,
notes the time on the clock
and walks away,
the ghost finally emerges from the closet,
but finds they are unable
to crawl back into the body they once called home.
They are unable to get back up again.
But they remain.

There's a phantom chorus
singing a sunny day
through these same dismal hallways—
light-hearted,
child-like,
carefree
and careless,
to remind us all before it's too late—

ashes, ashes.

We all fall down.

THANKSGIVING 2005

They said he couldn't come to dinner.
My uncle was too sick.
As we all gathered around to ask blessings on the food,
Grandpa prayed for him.
Prayed he'd have a good Thanksgiving anyway.
Grandpa has the best heart,
but I felt that prayer was pointless.

I had to leave early to get ready for work.
The graveyard shift,
which felt more literal than figurative some nights.
Before I went in, I drove the twenty minutes in the dark
past cornfields, Christmas lights, spinning tires and speeding sirens,
to see my uncle's daughter on her shift at the gas station.

You look upset, she said as soon as she saw me.
There was a terrible wreck on the highway on the way over, I replied.
How was Thanksgiving? she asked.
I didn't answer. Instead, I blurted out,
How's your dad?
My dad always brings him up randomly, I continued.
Says his biker friends threw him a huge birthday party.
Asks if he ever took me on that motorcycle ride he promised.
Says he's selling all his farm equipment because
he thinks this is going to be a really tough battle.

He has forty tumors, my cousin said. *In his brain.*
He has six to nine months to live. Could be less.

She looked at me, as my mouth went slack-jawed,
eyes grew wide
and a gravel rockslide formed in my throat.

You mean . . . you . . . you didn't know? she stammered.
I didn't know . . . how bad it was, I answered.

Does he ever ride anymore? I had to ask.
No. He can't, my cousin answered, looking down. *He just can't.*
She paused briefly, assessing my reaction, then continued cautiously.
We tried to come to your show last week.
He really wanted to. He was just . . . too sick.

Too sick . . . , I echoed.

Are you okay? she asked.
Yeah, I answered. *It's just that . . .*
there was a terrible wreck on the highway.

I left to go into work.
Why I schedule myself to work after family gatherings,
I have yet to understand.
God knows that these days,
especially this one,
I need a very stiff drink after family gatherings.

There was a terrible wreck on the highway.
An SUV swerved into the wrong lane.
The other car was upside down, crushed.
Shattered glass everywhere.
The ambulance hadn't gotten there yet.

TERMINAL

It's a path less traveled.
It's an end-stage fatal crossroad.
And the fork that lies across this junction
points neither left nor right,
but leads right to
multi-system organ dysfunction.

I think we know that this is terminal.
But we want to do everything we can
to add seconds to the second hand,
and save face
in front of fate.
Keep it together for family
despite the ICU insanity.

I had a fantastic time last night
as we took a hit
to that bucket list
and narrowed it down one by one,
like that last tropical vacation
before eternal sedation.
It ended way too quickly,
but my god, it was fun.

We watched our lives
flash before our eyes,
and we wailed and cried
the whole way home.
Not even a morphine drip
could get a grip
on loved ones lost
or time spent alone.

I think we know that this is terminal.
But we want to do everything we can
before this pain gets out of hand.
We have to save face
in front of fate.
Keep it together for vanity
despite
the ICU insanity.

FEBRUARY FIFTEEN

Things I wanted to tell you about my day:
—The dryer is fixed.
—The dog perfected his new trick.
—I started drinking at noon.
—When the maintenance guy came by about the dryer today,
I wanted it to be you standing at the door,
holding a cliché
like flowers or wine,
saying you were sorry for the way you left last night.

I wanted you on my doorstep.
I didn't want this to be the final scene.
I wanted you to be just like
the guy in the grocery store
buying flowers on February fifteen.

I wanted you
like a movie scene.
Except
I don't think you believe in movies
beyond what you can see.
There's a man
and a woman
staring back at you from a screen,
so you know that movies exist,
you just don't understand what they mean.

I let the maintenance guy in
and continue to wait.
For a moment.
For anything.
For fate.
For a phone call from someone so mean,
they thought that would be more rational
than flowers on February fifteen.

The dryer's fixed,
I wanted to say.
But it wouldn't matter.
It's not your dryer anyway.
You stopped believing in hope
because it's something you can't see.
I didn't mean to insinuate
that you'd ever have faith in make-believe.

The maintenance guy leaves.
He was nicer than you.
So maybe I should tell him
all the things I wish you'd do.

I wanted it to be you standing at the door,
holding a cliché
like flowers or wine,
saying you were sorry,
for the way you left last night.

Like believe in fucking miracles.
And all other things unseen.
Maybe believe
just a little bit
in me.
Be the knight in shining armor.
Be the hero of our movie scene.
And show up here with flowers
on February fifteen.

LET'S PRETEND

I am going to play pretend.

I am going to have cheese with my wine
and pretend I am classy,
like I did not just bite a chunk
directly off the block
with rogue crumbs
falling into lukewarm bathwater.

I am going to pretend
I am not sitting in lukewarm bathwater,
drunk at 1:30 p.m. on a Tuesday.

I am going to pretend
that canceled plans
are not metaphors in my hand
that I can squeeze
until the circulation is cut off.

I am going to pretend
that I will steal a spaceship.
Later in the week.
Maybe.
If I have the balls,
and if the stars align for the larceny of spaceships.

I am going to pretend
that in the days after you left,
it did not feel like
your brother dying all over again.

I know that when we were kids,
you don't remember the legendary chess game,
or the last time I saw him—
as he ruffled my hair
when he walked by the chair I was sitting in,
like maybe he was my friend,
and not just this cool, older kid I looked up to—
because you were playing outside.
When the two of you left that day,
it meant nothing.
And why would it?
It was just a normal Tuesday,
going home.
As if the day
would not end up a fateful memory
in any of our lives.

But I know you remember the haunted house.
The best day of pretend!
Grapes were eyeballs,
spaghetti were brains,
sheets hung like willowy curtains,
so that we could not escape into the daylight.
And I walked through the entire thing unfazed,
because I was a ten-year-old baller,
scared of nothing.

Your brother had made the spaghetti,
and he led us all the way through
the makeshift haunted house with an outstretched hand,
guiding us safely to the end,
as I felt he had years later
from the Other Side,
when you and I
were grown-up partners in crime,
who thought we could conquer the world.

But right now,
in this moment,
I'm going to pretend
that I haven't let down
not only the living,
but also the dead.

I'm going to pretend
that everyone eats cheese
in the bathtub on a Tuesday,
sobbing until the bath turns saltwater,
and I am perfectly normal.

And I'm going to pretend
that I have not made it
through real-life haunted houses
for real life
to be the thing that I am afraid of.

Because once upon a time,
I was all you ever wanted.

And in the background
of every adventure,
every fork in the road
a fleeting thought,
your brother's ghost would appear,
his outstretched hand guiding us
this way or that,
pointing toward the safe way through,
like he had never left in the first place.

And we were happy.
We were so happy.

Let's pretend.

And we were happy.
We were so happy.
Let's pretend.

KEEP TALKING

I thought that might be you.

The crowd felt like some surreal dream,
where you find all the familiar faces
you had forgotten about,
the ones your mind didn't need anymore,
the ones you thought you'd never see again.
The ones you were over.

We must have talked all night.
I'm surprised you had so much to say.
I guess it has been three years.
I guess it did end poorly.
I guess time heals all wounds.
I guess you're only in town for the weekend, so . . .
my place or yours?

You keep talking.
I don't mind.
I've never been held this tightly,
or felt this wanted in my life.
Even if it is just for tonight.

You say you wish you still lived here,
so you could see me again.

I don't believe a fucking word you say.

But keep talking.
It sounds nice.

EVE

Drown out communication
there's a silent salutation
when she can't look him in the eye
because she's afraid he'll see all the thoughts
she's been trying to hide

Dreading the evening
while biting her tongue
leaves history on repeat
and words left undone

Eve was made from Adam
from tiny ribs of bone
so she should obey his every breath
and not let the bruises on her own ribs show

Second best is relative
promises only tentative
he's waiting on something better to come along
maybe something ninety-proof
and very, very strong

Second Best can't feel pain
without being labeled crazy
while Number One sits in his glass
looking all burnt-out
and lazy

Of course Eve was made from Adam
from tiny bony ribs
so she should never question
his white lies and little fibs

Her heart can only say *last call*
so many times before it retires
and she's starting to read his mind
phone tapped like a wire

Second Best can't cry
without demands of why
and hands around her throat
squeezing tighter, tighter
tighter until she chokes

Course Eve was made from Adam
from tiny ribs of bone
so she should obey his every breath
and never let the bruises on her own ribs show

BUZZ

On the wall the clock ticks
falsely though, 'cause the second hand is stuck at six
I'd give anything for an evening of wasted time
though my fear of running out of rhymes
cripples my thoughts with every sip

But suddenly these lines
come flooding through my head
like white noise so soft
write it before the buzz wears off
write it before the buzz wears off

There's a silent tick-tock
from the wall clock
but it's an imaginary hoax
because the second hand is broke
a collateral victim of time's battle fought

There are a few things I never got to say
they hide in my brain's crevice corners from day to day
saving themselves for a deathbed apology
or to turn back time chronologically
our last conversation rewound and on replay

All these words I never said
are stuck in my head
in the white noise so soft
say it before the buzz wears off
say it before the buzz wears off

Instead I found myself wallowing in regret
for the things I couldn't say yet
it's only your ghost with whom I'm infatuated
when my brain's slightly saturated
and so I reach for my cigarettes

And I've got the perfect song
I've got all the lyrics down
perfect for the exhalation
perfect for when your ghost comes around

But in between every verse
I know my memory is getting worse
in the background noise the words get lost
so
smoke it before the buzz wears off
smoke it before the buzz wears off

I catch myself in the reflective glass
smoke and mirrors play back
this face says all the clock couldn't say
every tick-tock closer to the grave
with these reveries burned down to ash

The past stared me in the face
with every word she had to say
whispered in the background noise so soft
live it before the buzz wears off
live it before the buzz wears off

I DIDN'T REALLY WANT YOU TO

I didn't really want you to say goodbye.

Instead, I wanted you to say
that you love the way my laughter
fills an entire space,
and that even when you're upstairs,
you know I'm here by the sound of it.

I wanted you to say
that I have the kind of allure
that when I'm sitting at the bar,
no one else is there.
Not because the bar is empty.
But because you don't see
anyone else.

I wanted you to say
that you love the way I sit on pool tables
even though it's against the rules,
that you love my faulty confidence
in a game of darts,
and my terrible karaoke singing.
These things must be endearing
to someone,
I'm sure.

I wanted you to say
that after the bar closes
on your last night in town,
we should grab a bottle of wine,
go up to the rooftop
and talk until the sun comes up.

But you didn't say any of that.

You simply picked up my receipt
as I climbed off the barstool,
wiped away the ring-shaped wine stain
I left on the bar,
said,
Shane will be behind the bar next week,
and left it at that.

No, I didn't really want you to say goodbye.

So I'm glad you didn't.

TAKE A PICTURE

Take a picture of me, I said.

We haven't taken any pictures all year.
And I'll smile,
I'll even laugh,
and then maybe when we look back,
we'll remember today as a good day.

The summer sun.
The inflatable pool.
Unbreakable wineglasses.
A day off.
A day we've been trying to have all summer,
but couldn't find the time.

Try to remember the good,
I tell myself.
Forget how heavy you feel today,
how heartbroken,
how defeated.

Forget the desire
to no longer be a part of this world.
Quell the voice in your head that says
no one would miss you
if you were gone.
Drown out the demons
holding court in your brain,
placing bets over how long it would be
until someone found your body.
Laugh them off.
No one will hear the rolling of their dice
over your trademark laughter.

Forget the stares from the outside world.
The under-their-breath comments.
The hurtful words,
the haters,
the extreme self-loathing,
the things that made today a bad day.

Remember the sun.
The pool.
The dog.
The smell of sunscreen.
The feeling of being child-like,
with no responsibilities
holding you down.
The feeling of being loved unconditionally.
Remember these things.

Forget what made today a bad day.
Immortalize what made it a good one.

Take a picture of me, I said.

9 P.M.

SEASONS

We don't talk about how dark this winter was.

When the obituaries were six patients deep
on a Monday morning,
we called it an easy weekend.
When we got through even just one shift
without breaking,
we called it a good day.
It's strange how relative
common phrases become.
It's strange how death
becomes so common,
we have to write off entire lives
just to get through the day.

I want to write about,
not write off.
Everyone deserves to be remembered.
Let me tell you
some stories . . .

Let me tell you about
the young father of four,
who did everything right
except for where fate intervened,
whose family missed his last breath
by mere minutes.

Let me tell you about
the doctor we coded
until her pupils were fixed and dilated,
and we knew
we had lost her.

About the virologist,
who died with no one at his bedside
but irony.

The World War II veteran,
who heeded all warnings
and took all recommended precautions,
but couldn't do a damn thing about
time not being on his side.
On his last day on earth,
he prayed to God
and predicted his own death,
accurately dying that very night,
taking with him
an entire century of history.

The man who was so afraid
to die alone,
but did just that—
on Christmas Day.

The 35-year-old
who never got an obituary,
as if there were nothing
in three and a half decades of life
to remember
upon departure from this earth.

The daughter, who spent all her time
taking care of her dying mother.
It can be a nasty little habit of caregivers
to forget to take care of ourselves.
Her mother died in hospice care.
Two months later,
she died on a ventilator,
drowning in her body's own fluids.

Notice something?

These stories don't have endings . . .

We are all born into industry.
Healthcare is an industry.
Funeral service is an industry.
You pay for your life,
you pay for your death.
That we leave this earth
with coins covering our eyes,
and are not born into it that way
is a major inconvenience,
and I think you know where this is heading . . .

These stories don't have endings.
Their last pages have been ripped out,
never to be finished,
and we only remember
what we pay for.

No, we don't talk about how dark this summer was.

You will choose
between breathing and eating.
Even prisoners get a last meal
before execution.
You won't.

Your struggle to survive
will be mocked on social media
by the laughing faces
that follow news articles.

These deaths will be heckled,
along with our every effort
to save them,
even though
the Angel of Death looms angrier
and more unforgiving than ever before.

Every day, a war.
Every day, we lose.
Every day, the laughter ensues
on media outlets,
stating that we faked these battle scars.

You cannot fake
puncture wounds from a scythe.
You cannot fake collapsed lungs,
ground glass
or the sound of someone drowning.
You cannot fake a flatline.

You think we ride high on job security.
You think there are not millions
of stories just like these.
You think there aren't people out there
breaking
every
single
fucking
day.
But do you think
we'll ever come back from this season?

No, we don't talk about how dark this fall was.

STORY TIME

Everyone's reality is different
so who knows which story is really true?
I wonder which has the better ending
the one by me or the one by you?

Course mine was a real cliffhanger
above the ground so soft
and it took every last dot dot dot
to keep me from jumping off

I hear yours is a real page-turner
but the ending's very blunt
and right after chapter seven
you say goodbye to us

It implies my own reality
from my library of perspective
is too complex to understand
and is far too reflective

You just skip straight to the point
and breeze past all description
state my character is too dramatic and
that's the author's dereliction

So we said goodbye to fairy tales
and all that warm fuzzy stuff
that's the problem with happily ever after
it can only happen once

You turned to the last page
to find the tragic flaws in ourselves
said the ending's not that great
and put our story back on the shelf

Everyone's reality is different
so who knows what's really true?
But I think the endings are the same
the one by me and the one by you

TODAY I WATCHED THE WORLD BURN DOWN

Today I watched the world burn down.
Saw the smoke cloud to my right,
and I just walked on by.

Looking back in retrospect I've always had a save-the-world complex
but it's gotten far too big for me and maybe I don't want to see this
world be saved every fucking day it's a media bullshit parade we've lost
our senses to our own defenses and now we can't even smell the smoke
from the latest bullet hole

Today I watched the world burn down.
Saw the smoke cloud upon my return,
and I just let it burn.

As an empath I can't let this pass it was once what's yours is mine
but we haven't missed a beat since Columbine and you'd think things
would be better since 1999 but '90s nostalgia feels like home and this
year alone we've got a map full of bullet holes so no
I can't love everyone anymore
not when the American dream starts to sound like folklore
not when last words
are to the cashier at the grocery store

Today I saw the world on fire.
I did nothing.
Let the flames creep higher.

All these things on the news but one day these tragedies will affect me
and you and not only me personally but people who were my saving
grace through the ages how easy it is to leave two kids without a father
as tensions get hotter over seeing things in black or white
come on, guys
this was someone's life
Over the last few days my heart has broken in ways I had never seen
before and mending it has become a daily chore after all these endings
the underscore as the credits roll up and I'm left sending love in a
plastic cup to people who are so numb
they can't even feel anymore

But maybe
if we stop giving the rat race Vitamin K let them bleed out their eyes
from day to day a little Warfarin for the war within and things like this
would never happen again I have my reasons to believe in humanity
but we're looking over the cliff of sanity and baby it's a long way down
to the ground to the flames the fits of rage to the violence and the
blind-eye silence but
off the cliff we go
and where we'll land
nobody knows

Today I smelled smoke.
And I just let it go.

SUNDAY MORNING CIGARETTE

Patent leather boots.
Black leather jacket.
Hey, baby, you dress so well,
it's hard for me to tell
all the things you're trying to hide,
and all the secrets you keep inside.

Hey, pretty girl,
you're dragging your feet.
But goddamn, baby,
you smell so sweet.

The *Come Fuck Me* boots
speak for themselves.
But I assume
that's what you were trying to do.
You don't hide so well.
Captivating love spell—
everybody likes it.
Everyone adores you.
Don't try to fight it.

Hey, baby doll,
you're a fucking wreck.
In thirty-degree weather,
there's really nothing better
than hot black coffee and a Sunday morning cigarette.

You need to leave soon.
You've got work to do.
So take that pretty little ass back inside
where you can find
yourself alone with your thoughts
in a mind that rots
behind a stellar Glasgow smile
that you've had carved on for a while.

He thinks you look at him differently today,
like you've got something to say.
You've got a lot of things
hiding in the wings
of your burnt-out mental center stage.
Yet these you keep quiet.
He's left you no outlet
except evident breath
from your Sunday morning cigarette.

Hey, pretty girl,
you're dragging your feet.
But goddamn, baby,
you smell so sweet.

You've got a lot of things hiding
in the wings of your burnt-out
mental center stage

ONLY IN THE MOMENT

It's been a while
since I've seen your forced smile,
and watched you walk
through my front door *just to talk.*
But that's okay.
We've seen it through.
And I'm running out of words that rhyme with you.

Do I ever get tired
of being the one they all want
because I want nothing in return?
I light your match,
I watch it burn.
But once fire hits my fingers,
I'll be done.
It didn't mean shit to you,
but you can't say it wasn't fun.

I've got three dates, but no time.
All these clever circumstances, but no rhyme.
You know your time has run out
if the words don't fly from my mouth
and scatter all over the page,
you know it's time for you to fade.

It doesn't matter how much you believe
of these half-truths,
if you ask what's on my mind,
baby, it's always you.
Though I'd never say that out loud.
I'm far too fucking proud.
But if I put you down on paper,
and I completely own it—
know you're in the moment,
baby.
But only in the moment.

REST ASSURED

I feel I could write a thousand words,
but all I've got stuck in my head
are the lines I've already said.
I'm so bored with you.
You're just déjà vu
and flaming hoops and circles
to jump through.

I thought we'd be home
all alone,
except for a fleeting moment—
your eye's on your phone.
And I knew it was her
from your deadbeat tone
saying the words
I have to go.

Don't worry about me.
I'll be just fine.
I have my wine,
my poetic shrine.
I rest assured in the knowledge
that you'd never leave her house for mine.

The fact that you returned
kind of makes my stomach churn,
like chalky liquid charcoal
coughing up lessons I had learned.
But I let you in
to start again,
like nothing even happened.
The match I lit fell deep in
as the water slowly churned.
Guess it's not time
for this bridge to burn.

So don't worry about me.
I'll be just fine.
I've got my wine,
my poetic shrine.
I rest assured in the knowledge
that you'd never leave her house for mine.

TASTY LITTLE POISON

The last three men
that have expressed interest in me
have either:

A) Expressed interest in many,
many other people as well.

B) Gotten bored of his wife
(too bland, he says), or

C) Didn't like the mail-order bride
he received and is looking to trade in
for a fresher model.

All this makes me wonder
if I have a half-lit, blinking neon sign
that screams *WHORE* on my forehead
that I'm unaware of,
all modern-day Scarlet Letter and shit,

makes me feel like I'm somewhere
between *good enough to be the other woman*
and *just not good enough,*

makes me look like someone's
leftovers.

And I realize
I am not as good cold
or reheated from the night before.

That the first taste
is always the best
and now you've had your fill.
I will sit here for weeks
waiting to be consumed completely,
the fear of being thrown out
ever looming.

So frequently at night,
I see you from the inside—
standing with the refrigerator door
wide open,
complaining
that there is never anything to eat
in this house.
I've learned to use this
lukewarm eligibility as a weapon,
because by now I know your tastes.

I know you wish
I came with a labeled expiration date.
I know you wish you knew
exactly
when this would be over.

As it stands,
you never know
when I will start to turn poison.

You'll think I look fine on the outside,
have a taste
and walk away,
while your insides are left bleeding.

With all these bad habits,
you were bound to get sick at some point.

She looked so good, though, you'll say.

So good, but was it worth it?

This half-lit midnight snack.
This tender little morsel.
This tasty little poison.

PRETTY PLEASE

I hear you're looking for me
sapphire eyes, ruby lips so pouty
and something sinful on the tongue
all for Your Majesty's bounty

But once you hear
all the things I have done
I'll never be your queen
you'll know I'm not the one

I've never been a beggar
but you want me on my knees
so you can forgive all my sins
down to one last pretty please

I've never been a chooser
and I wouldn't choose you either
the less saintly I become
the more I'm not a people-pleaser

But I can play this up
I can embody lust for you
and it'll be up to you to decide
if you think I'm telling the truth

You can pick your sin
because I can play envy too
whichever one you prefer
whichever looks best on you

All your chosen greed
tugged at my heartstrings
until they ripped to pieces
and were strewn all over things

But all the king's horses
and all the king's men
couldn't put them back
together again

And they all ran with scissors
upon horses of thread
with mouths full of lies
'cause you think you're a godsend

Even though they feigned chivalry
they couldn't escape this tragedy
and I knew they were sent by you
you sorry excuse for Your Majesty

I'm brought here before you
for these sins I commit
though I'm certain I'm only here
for your benefit

All my accusations
you didn't answer
you were entertaining another
beautiful disaster

So I didn't bow my head
at your pitiful pride
I didn't ask for forgiveness
I asked for my demise

I've never been a beggar
but you want me on my knees
so you can forgive all my sins
down to one last pretty please

VELVETEEN

This much I'll reveal
I'm a pretty little plaything
but please be careful when handling
because it's me you're trying to conceal
like you know I'm not even real

I get shot down after every shot
but I'm level like the lever
on the thermometer that says scarlet fever
your forehead's so hot
your heart is not

I look at you, but I'm unseen
and I can't go near ya
for fear of being burned like bacteria
though the ignorance seems so mean
it's okay
I'm only velveteen

I'm not the real thing, you see
I'm not velvet
I'm sure you felt it
when you ran your hand alongside me
then said you had to leave

I haven't been loved enough yet
I'm always still seen as ugly
and I know you were struggling
to see someone else in this bed
feel her pristine, perfect velvet

Being with me brings full regret
maybe I'll be real another day
you leave me here with my malaise
fever breaks into a cold sweat
stains your pristine, perfect velvet

I look at you, but I'm unseen
and I can't go near ya
for fear of being burned like bacteria
though the ignorance seems so mean
it's okay
I'm only velveteen

GOLDILOCKS PRINCIPLE

I had a dream
that I was walking down your street,
and I got tired,
so I broke into your house all Goldilocks-style,
and you still lived with the three bears.

Even though
we all know
Goldilocks can be an entitled little bitch,
which
I know you believe,
you still came to retrieve
me out of your bed
and you said,
What did I do wrong?

These words, this phrase
echoed in my head for days
like a song
with that one line
you can't shake or define,
but when I finally got up out of your too-hard bed,
all was quiet.
So while the riot
went on upstairs to burn me at the stake
for the break
and enter,
I could answer.

If you could
crawl out from under this skin
you've made me so uncomfortable in,
as I'd prefer the goosebumps and wrinkled flesh
come from laughter all my own
and not your humdrum monotone.
Your happily ever after
is speechless nights spent at home,
leeching onto your too-hard bed,
and I can't get every compliment you never gave me
out of my head.

And me?
I'll answer the question without being asked.
I should not have gotten so angry so fast,
should not have felt things
or tried to breathe,
should not have come unhinged
or needed reprieve,
should not be so free with expression,
should not let insomnia take possession
and in the end, stay up reluctantly learning . . .

upstairs there's a
strike
hiss
sizzle
and I'm pretty sure the torches are burning.

I knew it was a dream at this point
because Goldilocks wasn't burned at the stake.

She was eaten alive.

Which . . . you did that too.

But I promise you,
when the time is just right,
I'll wake up in my own bed in the middle of the night,
in the perfect life
I've created,
I'll look around
and realize Goldilocks isn't as bad as she sounds.
Because I'll never be abated,
but I will evade
this deceit
and all beds made of concrete,
and believe me,
honey,
I will never again
dream of your street.

I will evade this deceit
and all beds made of concrete

IRONY TOWER (AN ELEPHANT NEVER FORGETS)

The elephant is back.

Midnight text message reads,
Moving out of state, but wanted to say goodbye.

Say goodbye.

This is strange
because you haven't verbally said anything
in over three years,
haven't virtually said anything
in six months,
when a text message you sent over Thanksgiving read,
Go Panthers!
And I wanted to respond with
Yeah! Keep pounding!,
but didn't,
as I realized this would be the
worst
thing to say to you.
You don't need the encouragement.

I lie awake and wonder
how many other carbon-copy blondes
also got this midnight message.
Wonder how long it takes
to copy and paste
a thousand ex-girlfriends.

Falling in love with you
was never part of our deal,
and I tried my damnedest
not to.

You were the first line of *Naked Truth*.
Don't flatter yourself.
It isn't a compliment.

You were the cracked glass
of *Faceless Mirror,*
the bloodstains on the carpet
from *Hemorrhage,*
and the horrid sappiness
of when I tried to write
a love poem.

You were the perfect muse
for a vengeance poet.

The thrill of reciting a poem
with the person it's about
sitting in the audience,
squirming,
not being able to do a damn thing.

But this did not happen.

The last time I saw you,
you showed up late
and incidentally,
after my set
which had nothing to do with you anyway.

As the musician on stage sang,
and I just conquered North Caroline,
I saw the Old Fashioned
out of the corner of my eye
at the edge of the bar,
with the elephant
sliding cash to the bartender.
I was distracted by friends,
fans
and beautiful people,
but you edged your way
into my eye's corner next to him.

And then I left,
applauding myself
walking by you
without saying a word,
because I just conquered North Caroline.
And I never heard from you again,
until this middle-of-the-night message of
goodbye,
to which I said nothing.

I know
I was never supposed to love you.
But I did.
I fucking did.

The elephant
leans on his barstool,
clinks the ice in his empty glass

and waits.

BULLET

It's been one hundred hours,
and I've heard nothing from you.
So I'm doing everything in my power
to keep from telling you the truth.
Every word I want to say
just loaded in the dock,
for the next time you get drunk enough to talk.
But I'm afraid to hit send
because that will be a permanent end.
All my metaphors cracked and coded,
my verbal gun
is fully loaded.

Course I shoot straight from the hip as these words leave my lips and
land around you but won't ground you the lack of sound proves that
you don't know what to say ever in the day to day I've got my bullet in
the chamber ready to aim here so you can bear my very last truth that
proves everything I ever said was aimed straight at you

I read my words again
and again.
Find the courage to hit send.
For final closure.
For this to finally be over.
But all my ghosts
keep looking over my shoulder.

When I was eleven a childhood friend went to Heaven so when I was
thirteen I started visiting the ghosts that visited me and even though
my father offered me a front-row seat in the cemetery I can't find anyone to come along for the ride even though I've tried with you once I
pull the proverbial trigger you'll be a ghost too and I've been told
I'm a really cute gravedigger

Word for word
may go unheard.
If my courage were bigger,
I'd pull the trigger.
But maybe there's nothing left to say,
and you'll live another day.
Yet in situations so dire,
maybe there's nothing left to do but
ready
aim
fire.

10 P.M.

AFTER SIX MONTHS IN THE TRUNK OF MY CAR, ON WHAT WOULD HAVE BEEN OUR ONE-YEAR-AND-SIX-MONTH ANNIVERSARY

I wore the silk you gave me for the first time.

I don't really know why,
but it was comfortable,
and I got to see me
exactly how you wanted to see me.

TALES OF TERROR AND HOLY MATRIMONY

I.

There was a knife you kept in your pocket.
You flicked it open and closed when you were nervous.
This, in turn, made me nervous,
especially when you stopped being able to make small talk
without your knife blade out.

I found out you were selling Vicodin on the streets.
I yelled.
Told you I was not okay with it.
Told you I was leaving.
To get me to stay, you held my throat against the wall,
your working-class grip strength slowly closing in.
I thrashed and struggled free.
Turned back to get the last word.
I just couldn't leave without the last word.
It was my only weapon.

You threw your open knife at me.
The blade glistened as it caught the reflection
of the kitchen's fluorescent light midair.
I jumped to the ground,
covered my head with my hands.
The wall garnered a new flesh wound.

II.

It was Valentine's Day.
We didn't want to wait at a restaurant, so we just ordered a pizza.
I said I wanted all vegetables on my half, no meat.
You said you were tired of my shit and stormed out of the room.

I followed because I had no idea what just happened,
other than that you must now deem me not only a burden to you,
but to the pizza guy as well.
You grabbed my shoulders and shoved me into the wall.
I kept hearing myself, as if from somewhere outside my body, shrieking,
What happened? What the hell just happened?!?
I broke free from the wall
as you lunged backward to gain momentum,
then you pushed my body away with all the force you had.

I grabbed your shirt to keep from falling,
but gravity was stronger.
I heard the sound of ripping fabric
as the side of my head hit the corner of the side table,
and I landed on my forearm at an awkward angle.
You made an incessant, cacophonous sound,
I couldn't tell if it was crying or laughing.
You ran out the back door,
and continued to run until you tripped
and collapsed in the snow, beating your fists on the ground.

I called your friends to come get you,
the ones who were security guards,
because I didn't want to involve the real cops.
You stayed with them for a few days.

My landing forearm bruised all over,
turning from black to shades of green and sickening yellow.
I took pictures of it, for *just in case* evidence
I knew I'd never use,
like your friends told me to.

I bought you a new shirt.
I knew it was your favorite.
I thought it was my fault.

III.

You went on Suboxone,
so I thought it was safe to marry you.
Even though I hid under my covers for hours
if someone wanted to discuss wedding planning,
and developed an instant crush on anything
that had a pulse and walked on two legs
into my field of vision.
Except you, of course.

It's just cold feet, I told myself.
Happens to everyone.
I thought it was perfectly normal.
I was told years later that it was not.

I don't remember this next part.
It was recounted to me much later.
I was drunk at my rehearsal dinner
because I didn't feel like dealing with it.

I do remember you kept cussing in my church.
Now don't get me wrong,
I'm a big four-letter-word fangirl.
But not in a church.
Never in a church.
Never in *my* church.
I told you to stop it—
asking nicely wasn't an option when dealing with this level of disrespect.

Shut up, you cunt.

I don't know how I got outside,
but suddenly I was,
and my wedding director was in my face begging,

Call it off, Amber. You don't have to go through with this.
You can walk away right now; you don't have to do this.

People traveled from a long way, I groaned.
I can't do that to them. I can't waste their time like that.

So the next day, I walked down the aisle.
Saw the altar ahead, focused on it to keep my balance,
the dizzying thoughts in my head on repeat—
You can get out if you need to.
This doesn't have to be permanent.
You can get out if you need to.
You can get out if you need to.

IV.

You never came home one night.
I knew you were seeing someone else.
You stormed in at 9 a.m., angry that I was home.
I asked where you had been.
You said it was none of my business.
I told you that I was your wife,
therefore, it was my business.

You lunged at me and I hit the wall,
the *thud* of the back of my head on the plaster
resounded in my ears like a small unpleasant buzz.
You punched the wall.
A new hole appeared.
You grabbed the Christmas tree and flung it across the room,
ripping the plug from the wall.
All the lights went out, and the room went dark.
Raging, you grabbed all four pillows, one at a time,
and threw them across the room.
You ripped the sheets off the bed,
stripping it in anger, and suddenly collapsed on the naked mattress.
You instantly went unconscious, and your breathing slowed.
I left for the day.
I never wanted to go back home.

V.

It was your birthday.
A family member of yours had died two weeks prior.
Coarctation of the aorta.
Closed flow to everything.
But we didn't know that then.
We just knew they never woke up.
Everyone just assumed it was a drug overdose.
I expected you to be emotional.
I didn't expect you to be homicidal.

On the way to the restaurant for your birthday dinner,
you laughed and you cried interchangeably
until it all sounded the same.
You took phone calls from your 19-year-old mistress during dinner,
while I pushed an onion around my plate with my fork.
Finally, I couldn't take it anymore.

Sometimes I don't even think you love me anymore,
I heard myself say.

I could have apologized for being petulant,
but you hung up the phone and glared at me.
You picked up your beer, emptied it onto your steak and my salad,
then stormed out of the restaurant.

At that point, I didn't care.
I finished my dinner, beer vinaigrette and all.
After all, I was the one paying.
You were waiting in the lobby.
You had accidentally locked the keys in the car before we came inside.
I called AAA, and in the 45-minute wait,
you threw your wedding ring in the trash and insulted me
in every way you knew possible.

You're a horrible kisser. I bet it's because you're fucking a doctor, you whore. And that makes you a horrible wife. And why don't you ever clean when you get home? You only work twelve hours a day. You have plenty of time.

Why don't YOU clean? I retorted. *You DON'T work.*

I'm the husband. I lay on the couch and drink beer. That's what the husband does.

When the mechanic freed the keys from the car, you took the wheel.
I thought nothing of it. You always drove us.
The radio came on, Ed Sheeran sang.
Before I knew it, you blasted out of the parking lot,
roaring past the speed limit sign that read 25.

I watched the speedometer creep up.
Fifty.
Sixty.
Seventy.
I yelled for you to stop.
I begged you to let me drive.

You laughed. It wasn't the laugh of a sane person. It was maniacal.
You white-knuckled the steering wheel, and turned a hard left
where there was no left turn.

The car spun in circles.
I grasped the door handle.
I screamed.
I closed my eyes tight and waited for the crash.
I told God I was sorry for being a bad person,
chanting in my head,
I'm so sorry.
I'm so sorry.
I'm so sorry.

I screamed again.
What was taking so long?
There was no stopping, no crashing.
Just spinning.
And then something strange happened.

Suddenly anything I had planned for this life,
on this earth,
meant nothing.
I knew I was going to keep going.
Maybe not in this body,
maybe not in this life,
maybe not like this,
but I was still going to be me.
As my own screams fell deaf on my ears,
I felt an immense peace.
Everything was going to be okay.
Death was nothing to fear.
Death was just a change of plans.
And it was so peaceful, how could we waste any life dreading . . .

GET OUT!

The car had screeched to a halt in a parking lot,
and I was being yelled at.
I immediately obeyed and opened the car door.
The entire sky reeked of burning rubber.

You got out too, and as I walked around the front of the car
to the driver's side, your path crossed mine.
You stopped, looked me dead in the face and said,
I wish I would have killed us.
I took the keys and drove us home.
The whole way you laughed.

How no one saw, I don't know.
How I am still alive, I don't know.

At home, you ran inside, laughing, crying
and ransacking everything.
I heard punches to the wall. I heard furniture overturned.
I heard the same song that was playing in the car earlier.
I heard screaming.

I stayed hunched in the car,
the very car that was nearly my coffin only moments before,
locked the doors
and made it my safe haven.
I stayed there until the screaming stopped.

When all was quiet, and I finally went inside,
you were passed out on the couch.
I went to the bedroom and locked the door.

When I woke the next morning, I knew I had to get out.
I had to leave. Forever.
If I didn't, I knew I would die.

Sometimes we break promises to God.
Sometimes we break promises to each other.
Sometimes we can count on one hand how many tries it takes to leave.
Sometimes we need many hands, taken from anyone who offers.

Sometimes
'til near death do us part is the best we can do.

DEATH PRACTICE

The choices I've made since you died,
I made with the best of intentions.
I wanted to save the world
because I couldn't save you.

When you had a seizure,
I just stood there.
At 22, I thought I should know more
of what to do.
So I counted your respirations
and pretended that was helpful.

I put a toy motorcycle
in the flower bouquet
I brought you in the hospital.
Weeks later,
they placed it by your head
in your casket.
This is how I know
you remembered me
for however long forever lasted.

The choices I've made since you died
are the stupid choices people in mourning make.
The ones that make us feel in control
and untouchable.
Like we'd never waiver, we'd never shake.
But control—
it's like life that way.
We think we have a firm grasp and so much time,
but it starts to slip without us realizing,
slowly,
until suddenly
we drop the line.

Every loss,
every spiral,
every death we watch
is practice for our own.
By the time we get there,
we should know
how to handle it alone.

I know I am good at this.
I've learned to handle death so well.
You see, the epitaph
is just at the bottom of the glass.
And I've been getting there
a little bit quicker with each pour.
I'm glad you asked—
yes, I will have one more.

The choices I've made since you died,
I begged you in the sky for advice.
How much are we to give of ourselves
on this earth
before we become the martyr in our own story?
Should we save the addict?
Save the adulterer?
The sociopath?
And when we give our life for all their sins,
will they remember us as a hero?
Or will we be remembered
as the burden who gave in?
Didn't do enough,
took the easy way out?
The burden they were better off without?

These choices in the past flash
in front of me,
it's like a movie,
but I truly
wish it would quit.
I've had enough of it.
The Queen of Damaged Goods
just wants her final scene.
So if you would,
bow your head.
Keep your eyes down.
And please remove her thorny crown.

The choices I've made since you died.

PERMISSION

When I learned that your father had died,
I asked a close friend
if I had permission to be sad,
which felt a lot like
asking engulfing flames
for permission to burn.

You had always accused me
of being overly emotional, though,
so I wasn't sure.

The night of his funeral,
I went to a football game.
For what right did I have
to be sad about it anymore?

It's none of your business, really,
I could hear you say.

And maybe you'd be right.
For what reason should I
be so invested
in someone else's tragedy?
What right did I have to tell a story
that wasn't mine?

Later that night,
I went down to the water,
waded into the current
swirling up to my ears,
and asked the riptide
for permission to drown.

To those who have had to mourn in secret,
I see you.

To those whose feelings of sadness
came on like a demon
that did not have the permission
for possession,
I hear you.

To those whose heart sank
upon hearing news
that shouldn't affect you anymore,
I feel you.

Today I lit a cigarette,
took a drag far too big for
the lungs of an ex-smoker,
asked for permission to cough . . .

and choked.

I went down to the water,
and asked the riptide for permission
to drown

FOR SOMETHING

I step out of the car
upon return from the bar
and find it isn't cold out.
Walking up the front steps—
key in hand, foot in mouth—
I feel I've finally sold out.
Her boyfriend's back,
watching TV in her room.
The light flickers under her door
as I enter mine, the empty tomb.

Drinking leads to drowning
which takes me down rivers
that remind me of you.
And though the current's thrashing
against the rocks and crashing,
there's still something I want to prove.
The echoes of these waters
keep beat with the tune you were humming.
And baby, that's gotta,
that's gotta count for something.

This man at the bar called me every name
except the one I was given,
and something about all this attention
leaves me high and driven.
But burning bridges and *Caution* signs
don't mark the paths they used to.
And all these river rocks along the way
just leave me feeling bruised.

I thought maybe a late-night last call
Sunday night would do me good.
Answer me or answer not,
I figured you never would.
But you called back before I could finish
the cigarette I was bumming.
And baby, that's gotta,
that's gotta count for something.

On the ride home,
so monotone,
the stoplights blinking red at me.
I finally pulled myself onto shore
up out of that shot glass sea.
The lights flicker in the window,
sure sign her boyfriend's home.
But it's nights like this
I wish the house were alone.

So much I will never tell you,
these thoughts held captive in my head.
I've finally reached the strength
and quiet at home in my bed.
Of the thoughts that escaped,
I think you and I can agree on one thing.
That this has gotta,
this has gotta count for something.
Gotta count for something.

HAPPY ENDING

To me you were like poetry
keeping parameter and perfect time
but we weren't careful, lost train of thought
and everything fell out of rhyme

We've chosen different paths
that crossed but now run free
yet I think it would be a happy ending
to know you still think about me

I write to you every now and then
but I couldn't tell you why
your responses are so disillusioning
you've always told the prettiest lies

In all you do, I wish you the best
you're doing great, I knew you would
but tell me, were there ever any happy songs
that were actually any good?

Even though our song has ended
there are melodies in my mind I host
but none are as daunting
as the friendly conversations I have with your ghost

We've chosen different paths
that crossed but now run free
yet I think it would be a happy ending
to know you still think about me

OUT OF AREA

I missed you tonight.

These days have been so lonely,
I've grown accustomed to just picking up the phone
and calling anyone I miss.

It was a sudden realization that I could not call.

If I tried . . .

The number you have dialed has been disconnected
or does not exist.

The person you have dialed has been disconnected
or does not exist.

Your number is still in my phone.
I can't bring myself to delete it.
Kind of like the voicemail you left me
on the night of your last birthday.
Feebly, with a shaking voice,
you left a message thanking me for the birthday card I sent you.
I never deleted it.
After you died, I listened to it repeatedly
because it was all of you I had left—
these sound waves,
this specific tone and key
that did not exist anymore except in my phone.

Ultimately, the voicemail expired and was abruptly gone,
like everything will be eventually,
but I wasn't ready to let it go,
and I could not stop crying.

Though sometimes, I think you still talk to me.
Reminders of you appear,
then disappear,
as if they were never there to begin with.

Because of you, I know what I'm doing with my life.
The day I was accepted into school,
I thanked you in a whisper,
wondered if you'd be proud,
then found a random *Congratulations* card in the checkout aisle.
Yeah, you were proud.

And I'm going to do it.
I'm going to save everyone who is in your old shoes.
I'm going to save the world.
I couldn't save you,
and it won't bring you back . . .

but I think sometimes you're still here.
Just behind the thinning veil,
across the vast horizon,
a long-distance call that's just temporarily

out of area.

LINES OF COMMUNICATION

Rig me up a hairbrush
on a broomstick.
I want to talk to you like an audience tonight.
I want to say all the things
I couldn't say
when we were face to face.
I want to tell you how I really feel,
followed by rounds of applause.

Rig me up a corded phone,
with your number on speed dial seven,
or give me the memory
of which digits were yours.

Rig me up the manners of a shy ten-year-old,
whose parents were raised in the '50s,
who was taught the telephone manners
of introduction followed by inquiry.
But please let me reserve
my Y2K teenage self,
and the satisfaction
of slamming phone to receiver
in the event of a prank phone call,
or the angry comebacks
not coming back
fast enough.

Rig me up a prayer.
Rig me up a séance,
a psychic,
a Ouija board.
Rig me up the cold breath
of no one over my shoulder,
but the sense of someone there.
Send me signs from Heaven,
if that's the only way for you to speak,
but make sure
you still hear me.
Make sure you still are
what you always were to me.
Show me that we still know how to speak
beyond telepathy,
and that you've always been
watching over me.

Rig me up a mic
and an audience.
Rig me up choirs of angels
guarding an empty seat,
and let me speak
with the tenaciousness of a ten-year-old,
who just learned a juicy secret
from eavesdropping on the other line,
mixed with the audacity of a teenager,
who knows not all secrets
are worth keeping.

FOR A MOMENT

Somehow, I found myself
lying on your couch at 10 a.m.,
sniffing a candle that smelled exactly like leather,
wrapped in a Carolina Panthers blanket
and covered in blue glitter.

And for a moment,
I knew this could be perfect
if you would let it.

But in the next moment,
I knew more certainly
that you would not.

So for now,
this is enough for me.

I've been meaning to let
perfection slide
for a long time anyway.

LOGICAL

If I could ask
just one thing from you,
it would be an explanation
for everything you do.
It all makes perfect sense,
but in my own defense,
logic doesn't look very good on you.

I'm taking these pills
to drown out all feeling,
and make the cells stop
all these senses from reeling.
If you'd ask today,
don't know what I'd say.
It's just day to day in how I'm dealing.

You just stand there—
all logic and reason,
refined and defined,
all heartbreak and treason.
I wish you never spoke at all.
You always made me feel so small,
and March always was
the end of my season.

To parallel all the liars,
truth stealthily finds a way in
and brings about the ending
before we have a chance to begin.
From the inferno Dante looked up,
saw our going was getting rough
and made me believe believing was a sin.

All reason comes around
trapped in your business sense,
and cancels the heartfelt
from this chain of events.
Spontaneity could show you how,
but even Xanax can't save us now—
your splintered memory smashed to pieces
when it finally went.

If I could ask
just one thing from you,
it would be an explanation
for these things that you do.
It all makes perfect sense,
but in my own defense,
logic doesn't look very good on you.

EX-SMOKER

I now write of cigarettes
as I once did ex-boyfriends,
in how badly I want them at 2 a.m.

In the silence.
The secret.
In the addiction

and the regret.

11 P.M.

YOUR ENTIRE GRAVEYARD

This is not my grief.
This is your grief.
But I'm sitting here making metaphors
out of the one thing I remember most
about someone much closer to you
than to me.

And then I present to you
my silly little similes,
all sacrificial and awaiting
your approval.

My minute to your decade.
My seashell to your ocean.
My ghost
to your entire graveyard.

FORECAST

Every time I hear the truth,
I think of you.
In learning to let go,
I hear your *I told you so*'s.
Laughing your smokey laugh,
cigarette butts the aftermath
of lessons well learned
until your memories turned
into thin air . . .
and now
your
laugh
is
everywhere.

Cancer's crashing like thunder
into wind, rhymes and blunders.
But it's almost summertime,
and things feel alright this time.
Yet with the loss of one life,
the world spins faster,
off its axis
and out of rhyme.

I remember the night death came to prove itself.
I took my cigarettes back off the shelf.
And the irony was not lost on me
that the passing that put you out of your misery
killed your killer as well—
shot it right back to hell.
And I just sat there thinking of rhymes,
and the suicide of time
that was left on your clock
the moment it stopped—
when you met your fate
but escaped the pain.
Your last breath
put those years to rest,
as you exhaled all the minutes
that were left in it.

Cancer's crashing like thunder
into wind, rhymes and blunders.
But it's almost summertime,
and things feel alright this time.
Yet with the loss of one life,
the world spins faster,
off its axis
and out of rhyme.

THE ENDING OF A GHOST STORY

Every story has an ending.
Even a ghost story.
And from every story,
we learn many morals:
Love does not conquer all.
If things are meant to be,
it is only for a time.
And the most mourning you will ever do
will be for those who are still alive.

Here is the real story,
and it is mostly true,
depending on who you ask.

We went on our second date
the night Sarah died,
and I met your dog
(and even though she would love
this next line,
Sarah is not the ghost in this story).

I was so worried about
how much cleavage
was appropriate for your
dead childhood friend's brother,
but the general consensus
of people I'd asked was *medium.*
Which was really sound advice,
because the cleavage worked out great.

The night I dreamt about your brother,
he led me up to the porch
of your childhood home.
He gestured his hand
toward the open front door,
with a telepathic message saying,
Welcome home, kid.

And I don't know
if you and I ever quite made it home,
but I do know
that we conquered the world.

We put photos on the wall map
of every place we had traveled,
until the pictures congregated
and clustered sloppily
in some places we'd visit often.
Don't worry, you had said.
We'll get a bigger map,
as if the whole world itself
was not big enough to contain us.

I never needed a fairy tale.
But my own damn ghost story
doesn't even have a happy ending.

The night you left,
I did not sleep.
I laid awake,
writing lines I don't remember writing,
like the dreams you scribble down
upon awakening
before they are gone,
like the ghosts whispering
fleeting thoughts in your ear
halfway between sleep and dreaming
that you'll never get back.

All I'm left with are chess pieces,
heads-up pennies
and spaceships,
but to the untrained eye,
none of these things resemble a haunting.

Maybe your brother
just wanted you to have a taste of
what he never got to have,
maybe he was trying to guide us home,
or maybe I make too many decisions
based on whether the ghosts
will be angry with me.

But how *does*
a ghost story end?
Does the ghost cross over?
Do we put out the campfire?
Or do they just stop visiting—
with nothing left but a few knocks
at memory's window
every now and then,
or a faint shuffling across the brain's floorboards?

Maybe we bury the map.
Make an X in the dirt with a stick
over the final resting place
of the treasure of us,
for another to search for by candlelight
years from now to find
long-ago legacies
and the ending of our ghost story.

But for now,
blow out the candle.
Say good night.
And when you think you hear us
in the back of your mind,
tell yourself,
Don't worry.
It was probably just the wind.

Welcome home, kid.

STAR-CROSSED

Shakespeare's tragedy,
Romeo and Juliet—
after all these years,
I still haven't read it yet.
I'm not a big fan of what's popular.
Not big on being like everyone else.
But I'm big on martyrdom,
big on giving everything of myself.
I always thought it sounded so cliché,
but it seems I'd give my life
to be just like them anyway.

I talk to you
like *Taming of the Shrew.*
You try to clip my wings
by saying all the pretty things.
But this time I find
I can't be a martyr for you.

Like a star shooting across the sky,
irony falls.
What's left of our future
just slammed into a brick wall.
The stars never aligned
keeping us in mind,
and if celestial beings say no,
there really is no hope.
Only Romeo and Juliet
would understand this loss—
being damned from the beginning
and so completely star-crossed.

Merely uttering *Macbeth*
would mean certain death,
but even if we spin around three times and spit,
we still couldn't fix it.
On this midsummer night,
nothing comes out right,
and we can't make a sound.
The only thing one can hear
is the falling star
crashing
to the ground.

Like a star shooting across the sky,
irony falls.
What's left of our future
just slammed into a brick wall.
The stars never aligned
keeping us in mind,
and if celestial beings say no,
there really is no hope.
Only Romeo and Juliet
would understand this loss—
being damned from the beginning
and so completely star-crossed.

OLD LETTERS

Sifting through my email inbox, in an attempt to clean out all the *Your package has been delivered!*s, I found myself wandering down a tangled web of rabbit holes; each click leaving me to feel more and more like Alice venturing through a virtual fucking wonderland of her past.

As with most virtual rabbit holes,
I soon discovered that these should never have been explored.

In the cluttered cobwebs of old emails, undeleted from years and years prior, I found myself recalling missed text messages, weaving through saved AIM conversations and remembering words lost in the air—all from different mentors, friends, exes and dead people.

It felt like attending my own funeral. It felt like my life flashing before my eyes in Times New Roman type font, as one funeral patron after another brought my attention to . . .

September 24, 2001
You were my rock. I could count on you no matter what I did or what happened in my life.

September 30, 2001
Amber, I see a great potential in you, and a need for attention from men is not what is at your core.

March 24, 2003
Every guy wants a little . . . strange. And it's not about you. But trust me, Amber, you don't want to know anything else.

July 27, 2005
You should know by now that your unique mixture of heartfelt and smartass is one of the things I like most about you. We're lucky to have you around.

August 17, 2005
I can't explain it, Amber, because I don't understand it. If I were your age, I'd follow your little feet wherever they'd go. But I guess that's what makes the world go 'round, right? Different people.

December 29, 2005
I guess that's what you are there for—to console. You've got a big heart.

February 12, 2006
It's 2:30 in the morning! Where is Amber? Shouldn't she be here by now?

March 3, 2006
Goodbye, Amber.

March 6, 2006
You've put yourself through a lot lately. Not only with your uncle's health, but your job and where you want to live. Sometimes you just run out of tears. Once you get past the burial, you'll be okay.

June 7, 2006
Dude, have a rockin' day. Lighten up with everything already. Who cares what labels anyone tries to pin on you? Do what makes you happy.

September 13, 2007
I know you don't want to label this, but you belong to me.

April 9, 2008
That slice in your wall? That should not happen!

February 14, 2009
Take pictures of any bruising. Even if you don't use them now, save them. Just in case. Take time to clear your head, let this blow over. He can stay with us for a few days.

December 29, 2010
You think you're ever going to hack it as a nurse? You don't have what it takes! Stick to something that doesn't care. Stick to vegetables.

October 7, 2011
Amber, you don't have to go through with this. You can walk away right now; you don't have to do this.

November 20, 2012
You may want to check your husband's text messages. There are multiple times he has gotten a hotel room with this girl, so you may want to check bank statements also. One personal account has them having sex during class in one of the school planes, with the help of his friends watching out for them.

January 31, 2013
You're a horrible kisser.

January 31, 2013
You're a horrible wife.

January 31, 2013
I bet it's because you're fucking a doctor, you whore.

January 31, 2013
I WISH I WOULD HAVE KILLED US.

February 3, 2013
He did WHAT?!? Is he on drugs? I know there's always a he-said/she-said, and the real story is somewhere in between . . . but my god. Leave, Amber. Just leave.

October 27, 2015
You were always a godsend. And I took that for granted.

January 27, 2016
You will never get married again because that's how you are, Amber. You get bored of people, and you're a whore. And I don't care. I don't give a fuck. Childish? Sure. But I never want to see you again, ever. For the rest of my fucking life.

January 29, 2016
I had fun last night. Hope to see you soon.

UNLIKELY

When your life flashes before your eyes,
will I have made enough of an impact
to make an appearance?

LITTLE LOST CHILDREN

I. Cops and Robbers

Just last week,
there was a story all over the news
about a man who shot a cop four times
after a high-speed chase,
then turned the gun on himself.

Miraculously, the officer survived.

The suspect did not.

My boyfriend shows me
an old mug shot of the suspect
that was included in the news article
and asks,
Do you recognize him?
And as he places thumbs
to each side of the suspect's face
to cover the disheveled,
I see a child's face.

A child.
About five or six years old,
who came to my brother's
birthday parties.
A child
who brought a birthday gift
and ate cake and ice cream,
just like everyone else.
A child
who played pretend with his friends
in our backyard.

And I wonder,
did they ever play
cops and robbers?
Wonder,
did he ever ask to play
the bad guy?
Wonder,
was this crime
just an imagined scene,
played out so many times
all those years ago?

My mother never let us
have toy guns,
so as far as cops and robbers go,
we were unarmed.

But someone always has to play
the bad guy,
and I questioned
if he had rehearsed
to play this role his whole life,
starting
in our childhood backyard?

For if there are angels
walking among us
here on earth,
who's to say
there aren't also monsters?

II. Murmur

Your friend's obituary
was printed on the anniversary
of your dad's death.
I didn't know if you had seen it,
but was afraid of what you would do
when you did.

Checking up on you
via text message,
I asked how you were doing.
I'm okay, you wrote back.
Just thinking about him.
Thanks for checking in.

And by *him,*
I knew you meant your father,
not your friend,
and suddenly I realized
you didn't even know
he was dead.

The consequences of IV drug use
include severely broken hearts.
The broken parts
can only be fixed
and replaced so many times
before the break
becomes irreparable.

I never told you he was dead.

I'm running out of ways
to fix yours.

III. Strawberry Fields

As I walked down
the hallway at the hospital,
I peered into the room
you had been assigned.
All I could see were your shoes.
Facing upward,
like you were lying on your back
with nothing better to do
than count ceiling tiles.

And this would be a great reverie
if I had some memory
of your shoes.
But I don't.
All I have
is the memory
of the seventh grade,
you singing
Strawberry Fields Forever
in my ear
and a myriad
of unreturned phone calls.

These fleeting moments,
we don't realize
at the time
how they will
memorialize themselves.
How paths can cross
intermittently
for years,
then stray away
forever.

You were on suicide watch that day,
and how desperately
I wanted to go in and talk to you.

But isn't it strange to say,
Hey, I haven't seen you
in twenty years,
but I don't want you to leave.
Please stay.
It's not yet time for you to go.

So I didn't.

You were my friend's patient that day,
and I was worried
you might not want visitors,
or as it were,
yet another nurse in your room.

So I stayed out.
I kept my path running adjacent
and right next to yours,
but ensured that they
did not cross.

To this day,
I regret this.

If anything ever happens to you,
I will always regret
failing to save you with these words,
and not singing back to you,
Strawberry Fields Forever.

JUST WATCH THE FIREWORKS

I meant to pay bills,
but ended up writing instead
because 79.95 to the cable guy
gets nothing out of my head.
I knew this day was coming,
and my gut filled up with dread.
Not like it matters.
Just watch the fireworks, you said.

I respond in single-word phrases,
and use exclamation marks
you probably know I don't mean.
So you'll think I'm okay,
and that memory is nothing more
than a bad dream.
But I remember birthdays,
death days,
all the days in between.
I remember everything
everyone said on Tuesday,
even the things they didn't mean.

Today I feigned flawlessness,
poured vodka in my water bottle
just to keep me going
while my brain's going off full throttle.
I get so tired of trying to be perfect,
I can't even stand it.
To live up to the whole world's standards
and yours when you demand it.

Maybe I should have eaten something,
but decided to drink instead
because no amount of nourishment
will ever get this out of my head.
I knew this day was coming,
empty stomach filled with dread . . .
doesn't matter.
Just watch the fireworks, you said.

MUNDANE DAYS

What of all this time?
Minutes that don't matter?
This nothingness that fills
the blank space between
here and then gone?

What is the purpose of
each insignificant day?
The days the sun rose and set
without incident?
The daily bus ride home—
face pressed flat against the window,
breath staining the glass,
staring.
The monotony of the dripping faucet
no one ever bothers to fix.
All those hours spent
at red lights.

Do we live these days
only to surround the extraordinary
and the awful?
To take up space in our lives?
To kill time
until the next meaningful event
we are not likely to forget?
Like the phone call that sank your stomach.
The evening you were so happy,
you didn't want the night to end.
The time you thought you were madly in love,
but weren't.

But even these magnificent moments
are mundane.
They happen to everybody,
tediously placed in between
the moments too insignificant
to be recorded into memory,
or over the ones that are easily erased when
something bigger needs to take up space.

Erasure of memory means nothing.
Fleeting thoughts
turn into fleeting days,
and sometimes I forget who I am.
Mundane days leave no mark,
but take up so much time in the life,
and now suddenly
I am obsolete.
Aging.
Fading.

I cannot use metaphors today.
Time feels so literal
and ticks so loudly, but
nothing meaningful will happen.
Nothing will be recorded into memory.
So in time I will forget
that today I forgot
who I was.

EASTER SUNDAY

Bedroom balcony, April 12, 6:43 a.m.

I sit here waiting for the sun.

As if my insistence on stagnancy could prevent times from changing.
As if I could have my Easter morning as per usual,
with coffee,
the gravestones,
leftover foil-covered chocolates in the dewy grass
the children overlooked the day before
and the sun.

As if this morning,
there was not the hum of the dryer in the background.
If by chance, the clouds had not come up first.
As though the drizzle were not smearing the words
as they are being scrawled on this page,
like they should have stayed a messy memory,
never written.
And as if I were not out of coffee,
for my cup doth not overflow.

I didn't even know about the cancer.
I berate myself for being distant,
as the miles I've traveled on my own road
have never been far-reaching enough.
But your death,
on the same day as Jesus's,
should be poignant enough for this story.

I had grown used to the presence
of everyone I had ever grown up with
gathering on Easter Sunday before dawn
and gazing off into the horizon.
The hardened cemetery dirt signifying finality
of those who had gone on before,
as the sun flickering off the tombstones
whispered new promise.

But now
the rain pours.
The dryer sputters.
I see my own street below,
an asphalt prison I have confined myself to.
For here, the sun has not risen.
Indeed,
but I'm sure it must be rising in the cemetery.

And the dirt,
usually packed and grown over,
is soft and malleable,
having been disturbed with the offering
of one more body,
all sacrificial of childhood memories,
foil-wrapped candy
and kindness,
as the ground accepts one more of her own
in the burial of promise
and presence
on earth
as it is in Heaven.
For thine is the kingdom,
and the power,
and the glory,
forever.
Amen.

BUDDY, MY UNCLE, AND MRS. H

There's no one at home in the basement,
so I thought I would scribble tonight.
But it feels like nothing is wrong,
so I'm afraid I have nothing to write.

I used to read your old letters when I had nothing better but at a much
greater risk I read my old poetry to make sure I'm still good at this
haven't really felt like myself the wine's on the shelf and it stays there
for days like my notebook these days I write out my monthly budget
which just doesn't cut it so I read on repeat blank page after page

You know, she was a really sweet lady.
I remember her
from when she was more alive than on Thursday.
But as death takes hold,
we all look the same.
Yellow.
Unblinking.
A body.
No name.

When I think too hard I remember a sight I wasn't supposed to see
I'm so glad they took you that night before they called me and I can
condemn the ghost of your cancer forever but never never never does
it answer
and I miss you
since death kissed you good night I've held my lips tight and we all try
in vain to remain ourselves to remain the same through tragedy you've
handed me so much truth from beyond the grave every time it rains
and not to
worry . . .
I always knew it was you.

How I love writing.
I love how there's nothing
in my mind at all,
and then I end up with a summary
of things I forgot
were in my memory.

You took your life when I was just a kid yet I remember it it's actually
my first memory as an adult and I know it wasn't your fault because
I understand such pain I just wish you had let the rain pass because
sometimes just sometimes the hurt doesn't last and now that's your
last memory of this life but on some points you're right . . .
there will always be pain.
In that way, we are all the same.

I had nothing to write tonight.

It seems this amnesia
fades on the page
until the end,
and I say,
Rest in peace, my friends.

CURFEW

SCRAP METAL

I did not die in this car.

I locked myself in it after the fact,
smelled its familiar burnt rubber,
and waited until the screaming
inside the house stopped,
and the walls and the plaster
could rest in peace.

It died before me,
as it should, I suppose.

Sometimes it's just hard
to let your safe havens go.

A DAY IN THE LIFE

1) Buy new lipstick.
—A really bright shade, one you wouldn't normally wear, one that's sure to garner you unwanted attention that defines your self-worth.

2) Run a 5K.
—Pound the pavement, at least, if there's nothing else to pound.

3) Read a book.
—Be jealous of the fictional characters who get a happy ending.

4) Light a match.
—Remember that you are ashes too.

5) Lie down.
—Count sheep, ceiling tiles, wasted years . . . count whatever the hell you need to in order to distract yourself from the fact that you will not sleep tonight.

Get up.
It's a new day.
Try again.

1) Support small business.
—You can always help someone else's livelihood even if you feel dead inside.

2) Listen to a CD from high school.
—It's good to get back to your roots and remember where your angry-girl lyrics stem from.

3) Write.
—It's the only way to purge your soul without leaving this earth and save yourself at the same time.

4) Clean your room.
—Just because your life is messy doesn't mean your room has to be.

5) Rest.
—Enjoy the nightmares because they mean you actually slept.

Wake up.
It's a new day.
Start again.

1) Talk to someone you've known longer than twenty years.
—They've seen you at your worst and still love you anyway.

2) Drink wine.
—Remember there's a little more spark after each sip.

3) Forgive thee thy sins of self-loathing.
—You were not meant to be perfect. You'd resent yourself even more if you were.

4) Sing.
—Poorly. Into a hairbrush. Remind yourself that you're still an undiscovered, off-key bedroom rock star.

5) Sleep.
—Still. No dreams. Silence. Peace.

Wake up.
It's a new day.
And remember, anything can happen.

ATELOPHOBIA

Reading my own words unleashes a new, unnamed fear.

As if living them was not frightening enough—
the car,
the cancer,
the heartbreak,
the multiple victims of life strewn in between these pages—
no.

Breathing them elicits a sharp chest pain.
Allowing them to escape
through the air
to a stranger's brain
is the same as implanting a tiny tumor
in the unexpecting,
a malignancy that will grow at an alarming rate,
with contagions
to poison my own thoughts right back.

This fear
is the brass knuckles of a passerby
in a bad neighborhood,
and the sickening blow to the stomach
you garner for saying hello.
It is the double-edged sword of wordplay.
It is the raw underbelly of a bleeding heart, exposed.
It is the atelophobia
of sharing your story at a five-cent admission rate,
met with demands for refunds.

But it is also
the bitter, burning, back-of-your-throat taste
of giving up.
It is the crimson blood-red of exposed insides,
the gut-wrenching truth of knowing you have nothing left to hide.
Nothing left to give.
And nothing left to lose.

In between every once upon a time
and each happily never after,
I splay my keys between my fingers,
sprinkle the page with curse words
and wait for the beating.

Then I exhale a sequel,
draw chalk outlines around the accusations
and call it self-defense.

BASE CAMP

You don't ever get over anything.

Instead, you hold on to trinkets of trials and tribulations,
thinking,
I'll just save this one thing.
Something to remember this moment of passing through purgatory.

You're wrong if you think trinkets don't get heavy.

You carry around pieces of all the people you ever loved,
every meaningless moment,
the mundane beauty you found on any random Wednesday night.
You carry the heartache,
the *what ifs,*
the *under different circumstances*
and the terrible timing.

And the worst part is this:
You loved every person whole-heartedly,
just in case they were the last person
you would ever love.
You carry the weight
of every way you were ever healed
and every way you were ever hurt,
and expect it not to get heavy sometimes.

In remorseful moments,
matches are lit,
ghost stories are told over the subsequent campfire,
and the trinkets are burned to ash—
now more compact
and easier to carry around forever.

You meant to scatter them, I know.
Handfuls of soot slipped through your fingers onto the floor,
but you just couldn't let it all go,
so you clenched your fists and held it tight.
You have named your brain Bunker,
called your heart Hoarder
and yelled at her to clean up her mess.
But you are not alone.

Because I lied.
I lied when I said it was strange
that he remembered me enough
to say goodbye after three years of silence.
The truth is, I was flattered.
Flattered that I was able to set up base camp
in someone else's brain,
and after all this time,
the fire pit was still flickering,
the amber embers tracing synapses so fast
they created a forest fire,
fueled by bourbon and the full moon,
contained by the sunrise.

And after all these nights of fighting fires,
I am still there,
the ashes of drunken nostalgias that will always remain
a spark,
a heavy consequence
of a cremation campfire that could never fully be extinguished.

You are not the only one to carry the weight of heavy heartache.

Remember that we are ashes too, smoldering.
Laden in a corner brain bunker,
carried along forever by some,
the inextinguishable impact we made
that we may never even know.

Deny the past is over all you want.
Let go of the crossed paths,
the fleeting moments
and the haunts that let go of you.
But do not discredit yourself.
We all carry a little bit of each other around,
as an ember,
a spark,
a wildfire.

So let go of the shit.
Hold on to the sparks.
And know that you,
my darling,
fuel forest fires.

PULSE

I have this strange habit
of feeling for the radial pulse
of a person
as I'm fucking them.

As if searching for
as many signs of being alive
as possible,
since it is such a transient state.

THE GHOSTS HAVE BEEN
QUIET THIS YEAR

The ghosts have been quiet this year.

***

At my second-grade Halloween party, my friends and I played a game.
We went out into the cemetery after dark
to see who could get the closest to any given grave
without getting scared.
And without standing on it, of course.
We knew better than that.
That was of utmost disrespect,
and surely the deceased's hand
would reach out and grab our ankle,
and getting away would be the death of us.
To avoid this certain catastrophe,
we would jump over the ground
where the body was buried
and sneak up to the side to read its inscription.

Usually, a dog barking
or an owl screeching
would be enough to send us screaming
back inside the church
before we even had a chance
to read the names and dates written in stone.

***

On the road leading back to my grandma's house as a child,
there was a blue house that always kept a candle burning
in the upstairs window.
Grandma said the people who owned the house
had a little boy who died,
so they always left a candle on in his window,
in case he ever wanted to come home.

My cousin and I lived and breathed this story for years,
obsessing over the fact
that we knew of a *real-life* haunted house.
We made up so many stories
about the house,
the candle
and the little boy ghost;
and told them over and over again
until we ran out of different endings,
calling each other out on repeat stories.

But these stories,
and all other kid things,
went silent
the moment you became one of the ghosts of my childhood.

***

Yesterday, on Christmas Day,
I visited your old house for the first time.
In every window, candles flickered,
all the way down to the basement.
I walked up the porch steps,
with an uncanny certainty that I'd seen them before,
and stepped inside.
The wallpaper hasn't changed since you've left,
and there was a wall phone from the '90s
that I desperately wanted to call my parents' home phone on,
just to feel the depression of the buttons beneath my fingers.
Walking in the hallway,
out of the corner of my eye,
I saw the stairs leading to the basement.
I could not turn my head to look,
but instead, without warning but instinctively,
jumped past the doorway
out of respect,
like eight-year-old me
not wanting to stand on someone's final resting place.

I talked with your mother for hours,
this beautiful woman my heart had broken for
years earlier,
and we did not talk about you.
We talked about faith
and family
and all things beautiful.
We talked of the strange experience
of being in a place you've never been before
but can somehow sense its history heavy with heartbreak,
like it's a place whose story you've been a part of all along.

To speak of a haunting without speaking of a haunting.
To convey without saying that people come back
to the people they knew.
To know that souls eventually come back home,
to the house that left the candles lit for them.

No. We did not talk about you.

But were you there anyway,
visiting,
listening intently
to the life you left behind,
and to the people who keep your memory alive
to this day?

❈❈❈

The ghosts have been quiet this year.

This morning when I woke up,
I went downstairs and noticed
something off about the chessboard.
Something was out of place.
I looked closer, then I saw it.

Your favorite chess piece
had been moved from its original position,
had fallen down amongst its standing comrades,
your birthday penny normally housed underneath it
was now visible, shining and reflecting the light.

And I realized . . .

maybe I just hadn't been listening close enough.

To speak of
a haunting
without speaking
of a haunting

SUNLIGHT IN THE CEMETERY

Crossed over through the archway
to the dates, names and times—
none of which were mine.
But they're solidified in stone
and have gone on before.
How could one ask
for anything more?

This morning there was sunlight in the cemetery,
and it's been so long since I've seen it shine.
So I breathed in every invisible drop
as if it were all mine,
and I ventured deeper.
Six feet at a time,
I let my mind roam.
And for the first time in a while,
I started to feel at home.

Though I trespass on this territory
that is everyone else's,
I walked through
those graves so selfless
that if anyone saw me,
they'd think I was a ghost too,
just out for her 6 a.m. stroll,
with nowhere to go
and nothing better to do.

There was sunlight in the cemetery,
and it's been so long since I've seen it shine.
So I breathed in every last drop,
as if it were all mine.
With every step on dewy grass,
I let my mind roam,
and I felt one with the ghosts that stayed there
because they couldn't leave home.

WAITING ON THE SUNRISE

I opened a bottle of wine off the special shelf
because tonight is the last time
I will ever be able to drink good wine in this place.

And maybe that's a celebration to some,
but this wine bottle has stood like a fly on the wall
and watched the past five years go by,
and she's sensing a soon shattering
of her glass house.

And I do not know why
I have not yet learned
to build a home inside myself.
Why I must have four walls
and silence.
Why I have not learned that thus far,
I have survived everything
with solely the encasing of my integumentary system.

What I have learned . . .
I know why ghosts haunt their houses.
I know that the darkest hour is just before dawn.
And I know how much I love that dark hour.

But you have to understand,
the sun shines differently here.
And if you look into the clouds at dawn,
you can see everyone you've ever loved
shining back.

Sometimes, on the days the sun does not rise,
you find all your ghosts shrinking back
into your surroundings,
and you know that you cannot
leave them here alone.

Trust me, I know why ghosts haunt their houses.

This evening,
I let the water from the faucet
trickle down over my hands
as I washed away the expensive wine
I poured out for my phantoms,
and it felt like pieces of myself
were joining them here permanently,
washed down to the foundation
to remain in this house forever,
a suicide of cells
who would rather haunt these four walls
than carry on,
the longing to become
just a remnant in this place they call home.

In truth, I am my own thing that goes bump in the night.

I am my own shadows
lurking,
the ghost that haunts my own house,
until I wake up panicked and shaken,
and call it all a bad dream.
Tell the skeletons in the closet
they've got nothing on me,
'cause I'm waiting on the sunrise.

Explain that it's not that I don't still love the dark.
It's that I've learned to wake up on the other side of it—
where glass bottles line the shelves
and watch life play out,
and washing my hands is not
washing myself of the person who once lived here.

And tomorrow when the light finally breaks,
I'll step outside, suitcase in hand.
I'll look toward the sky,
and the ghosts of fleeting memories
will appear in the clouds,
waving silently,
a perceptual message coming down through the rays
to remind me that the sun will still rise
wherever I go.

EVEN THE MIRACLES

Starting another evening
with pouring wine down the sink,
saying, *this isn't just for me.*

Beating cancer once is hard.
Beating it twice is a miracle.
He was a miracle.
But that's too bad because you don't believe in miracles.
I digress.
It's okay.
They only last a short time anyway.
And by now,
all the miracles I know
are dead.

I used to say to myself,
I hope your next girlfriend is afraid of water
because then she'll never really see you happy.
Unless, of course, you drown yourself by other means.

But in the art of letting go,
I learned that the perfect vengeance isn't the answer.
It's not even the question.
What I really hope . . .

I hope she's good at death.
Not good at doing.
But good at dealing.
Not good like me.
In the way I say we're all killing ourselves
from the inside out,
the way this body rots itself
(as I talk about gangrene over breakfast cereal),
the way our cells
turn on themselves
while we're busy living,
how the cancer's coming to get us all . . .
and the coronaries so fragile,
they make a broken heart
a double entendre.

I hope she knows all the right words to say
to someone who will never say them back.
That she returns to you all the silence you need.
That she keeps you from spiraling
in a way I never could.
And that she's a really great funeral date.

My words,
my beliefs,
could never help you.
What you repressed, I amplified.
What I believed, you discounted.
And it's so hard to keep an atheist locked in a haunted room.
So when you get out . . .

I hear Heaven is a beautiful place.
And the people who've had near-death experiences
want their time of death to be called in that instant,
because the light is so bright, and all their friends are there.
That there's sparkle
every time God breathes,
and they would give anything
not to come back to this world
where we eat each other alive
and floss our teeth with the tears of heartstrings.

It tears my heartstrings to know
that the ghosts will never pick the candles for your birthday cake,
or send you greeting cards
in the checkout aisle.
Or trigger the unset alarm on their watch
at the exact moment of death
to prove to you
that energy really is neither created nor destroyed.
But they won't.
Because you won't believe them.

They come to visit you when you need them,
whether you know it or not.
And God is the hall monitor
who hands out permission slips,
or the parent who leaves the porch light on and says,
Just be back by ten.

Death is not the end.
Death is a temporary letting go.
You'll see him again.
And somewhere, there is beauty in all of this.

I believe
I am visited in my dreams.
I think the departed can reach us
through the thinning veil between dimensions.
And that coincidence
is just a fancy word for God.
I know
that when I go,
I'm going to rip out of this self-deprecating body
in an explosion of lightening,
and when I see the glittery exhalation of God,
all the beautiful people I've missed on this earth for eighty-some years
are going to be standing there,
being the shadows they cast in it.

Even the miracles.

What I really hope
is that one day,
you uncover a beauty like this
all your own,
and it brings you peace.

FINAL WORDS

I do not want you back.
I do not want you in my life.
In truth, I can't even stand
to look at you.

The only part that I'd want back
is the you I thought was perfect.

But that isn't possible.

Because you didn't fall from grace.
I discovered my self-worth.

PYREXIA IN THE TIME OF PANDEMIC

97.9

It's a waiting game,
knowing this will eventually come for you.

You see the news,
the politicians on camera
and Death's hyperbole,
knowing that Death can talk as big as it wants to
and regardless of timing,
will always follow through.

But you go to work anyway,
put on your armored face mask
in this new viral warfare,
and live your life.
Live each day just like any other,
and drink your wine,
which only dredges up
hypochondria's typical questions:
Are my affairs in order?
Should I scribble down a will on scrap paper?
What if I didn't live fast enough
to look pretty in my casket?

100.5

I think back to times of loss,
family emergencies and euphemisms
with the false positivity we always have.
Invisible missing faces gather 'round,
the holiday dinner table a snaggle-toothed smile of empty seats,
in a time when pain was supposed to bring about new growth,
but only harbored loss.

Wonder how long my seat will be empty for.
Wonder if I'll ever return.

101.3

I feel like my memories are being erased
before they even happen.
In May, I wonder what we'll do for Easter this year,
only recalling hours later
that Easter already happened weeks ago.

My father asks me to leave a spare key
outside my house,
in the event I don't wake up,
so I'm glad we're on the same page.
Sometimes I worry
my worst-case scenarios are too far-fetched,
so it's comforting to know
that this time it isn't.

102.4

Lining up songs for my funeral
just feels like choosing my open mic set list
for the week.
I pride myself on being the girl
who blasts punk music through the church cemetery,
and invites dead friends and family
to join the party.
They've returned the favor now
and are just waiting on my RSVP.

I check *Maybe,*
cross through *Plus One,*
and scribble on the side of the invitation,
Guys, look.
Near death is so much easier
when it happens in an instant,
rather than all this waiting.
Still not sure—
might have other plans.

103.2

I stand at my bedroom window,
staring down at the street
like a ghost who cannot leave;
the passersby unknowingly haunted
by my gaze,
as I steal a mental photograph
of a moment in their life
as they walk by,
a moment I was not meant to be privy to,
but only witnessed
because I lingered too long at a window
I should have left behind in the last lifetime.

104

I assume death
is something like dreaming.
And in my dreams,
I keep going—
forever aware,
forever cognizant
that I am me,
transcending dimensions.

I will still attend
my own funeral,
standing guard at the foot of my body,
and for those who believe,
I will let you know
I am there.

But once I am bored with ghostly games,
I will do what I've always done—
pull myself up out of the mess I find myself in,
shake off the ashes to dust,
and be the wraithlike phoenix
that visits in your dreams
when the time is right.
For I have never
been one to stay down for too long.

So I will rise above.
I will rise above.

I feel like my memories
are being erased
before they even happen.

DEATH WILL BE OUR CURFEW

Title by Christine Mello

It's crazy how when I recite these lines now,
I only need one book.

One book.

It's fucking laughable, really,
that all this time
could compress into 204
six-by-nine-inch pages.
What about the rest of the chapters
of our lives?
What about the chapters
we don't talk about?
What about the chapters
we edit out?

She went to sound check
down the street
before we exhumed
the past lives we had left buried
underneath the drumbeat.
If we crack the metaphors,
resurrect the apostrophes
and breathe breath back into
the curves of cursive,
we might be able to see ourselves
as we once were.

And even though
the music stopped hours ago,
we hung around like groupies
in our own backyard.
And maybe we should go inside
and be adults
with bedtimes
and curfews
and nine-to-fives,
but out here
we bleed more truth,
and out here
death will be our curfew.

Your ex-boyfriend
in the picture you showed me
now just looks like a middle-aged guy
with a wife and kids,
and maybe his honey-do list
on weekends is the best he ever is.
But I swear,
I saw him just a few months ago,
and it was the same scene
as when we were eighteen,
and not much else has changed, so . . .
picture perfect
doesn't always make it worth it.
We're better off out here
mocking the days of our youth
in this place where death . . .
where death will be our curfew.

We huddle under the stars
and our egos,
in the midst of the firelight
like we did long ago,
and we assign songs like business cards—
This song reminds me of you,
and beneath all your doubts,
this is who you really are.
This is who you are to me.
We will never be able to see
ourselves through each other's eyes,
but this is fine.
Because no matter how many chapters
we try to burn,
our lesson learned
is that someone
will always find us beautiful.

And all those nights under the stars,
we tried so hard to be responsible,
to be perfect,
to transcend,
when really
we just never wanted the night to end.

And as we stammer
with perfect grammar,
I realize I will never
be as beautiful in my own eyes
as I am to you,
on these nights when death . . .
when death will be our curfew.

ACKNOWLEDGMENTS

Thank you to my family, who has supported me even as I continue down the path with my potty-mouth poetry.

Thank you to my Lifers, whom I will always mention in the acknowledgment section of my books because I could never do this life without them—Christeeny, Lil Kirby & Big Kirby, Amy, James, Eric and all of Lost Friday—Britty, Branden & Branch—Trisha, Cuzzy, Gma, Sarah, Dustin, Lacy and Katie.

Thank you to Randy and Debe for being such avid readers and supporters.

And to Bre "Dr. Bossy," for always being willing to help with the logistics of bullshit.

Thank you to all the early '90s bands and artists, those who started out indie, those with the killer lines and the words that slay, those with stories to tell—Soul Asylum, Better Than Ezra, Ani Difranco, Jewel, Adam Duritz and all the Counting Crows. Collective Soul for releasing the only song Uncle Darrell "approved" of us listening to when we were kids. And Doug Hopkins, Robin, Scotty, Jesse and all of the Gin Blossoms for the songs and story that will forever stay with me. Combined, your words and music shaped my lyrical brain and will always make my little '90s-kid heart happy.

Thank you to everyone at Girl Friday Productions for your help throughout this whole process (and for making my life so much easier).

Thank you to Billy, for being my forever and ever best friend, for listening patiently when I answer the question *How was your day?* with things like *It was awesome! I FINALLY figured out what to do with that fucking comma!*, and for doing so much and being so wonderful to me no matter what ridiculousness I happen to be getting myself (or us) into.

Thank you to my readers, friends and audience. If I didn't have you, I couldn't keep doing this. Thank you, thank you. You mean the world . . . you have no idea.

OTHER TITLES BY AMBER SHOWALTER

The Carrion of Songs

Tender poetry with bite, a little salt and lightly peppered with profanity, Amber Showalter's debut collection takes the reader on a harrowing, yet heartfelt journey.

Esteem Punk

Disclaimer: This book was written by a 16-year-old emo-punk girl. In the year 2000. That's right, the poems in Amber Showalter's sophomore collection were actually written when she was a sophomore. In high school.

Both titles available from amazon.com.

ABOUT THE AUTHOR

Born to be a rock star but also born completely tone-deaf, Amber Showalter learned early on to use the written word as a weapon, as an epitaph, as her own spoken siren song.

A self-proclaimed type A personality and grown-up punk, world traveler and ex-model, Amber currently makes a living as a pandemic nurse fighting COVID-19, in addition to her crime-fighting side gig as a SANE (Sexual Assault Nurse Examiner). She has been writing poetry since she was fifteen. This is her third collection.

ABOUT THE ILLUSTRATOR

Viktoriya Samoylov is a Ukranian American self-taught artist residing in the beautiful Shenandoah Valley of Virginia. She is normally found in her home studio working on graphic design during the day, and painting in the evenings and on weekends. Her work consists mostly of impressionistic-style portraits in acrylic or watercolor, highlighting moments of nostalgia and light.

Viktoriya's work has been featured in *CandyFloss* magazine, Boomer Gallery in London, and numerous virtual exhibitions.

When not creating, she enjoys gardening, watching mystery shows at midnight with her husband, and of course, a proper cup of coffee.

Made in United States
Troutdale, OR
12/22/2024